To Tricie..—
— love Mama (2025.)
xxx

Copyright © 2025 K. Elizabeth Rose All rights reserved

The characters and events portrayed in this book are fictitious. Any similarity to real persons, living or dead, is coincidental and not intended by the author.

No part of this book may be reproduced, or stored in a retrieval system, or transmitted in any form or by any means, electronic, mechanical, photocopying, recording, or otherwise, without express written permission of the publisher.

Cover design by: K. Elizabeth Rose
Library of Congress Control Number: 2018675309
Printed in the United States of America

Jane's Weekend Antics

When Women just need a damn good laugh!

Written by K. Elizabeth Rose
Cover Designed by Symantha Myers

Chapter one

The morning after!

As the morning sun beamed through Jane's bedroom window she squinted her eyes, gave an exhausted yet refreshing stretch and instantly froze wondering, what the fuck was between her legs!

She laid very still..."*Well I don't remember that being there!*"

She tried to think of what happened the night before but her head was just a blur with no immediate recollections. As she moved her hand slowly down her body she felt this firm thickness of a manly thigh tightly in between hers.

Her hand paused, "*That feels nice, smooth skin… stop it!*" she thought, then each fingertip slowly raised up off his thigh one by one. "*What happened last night?*"

She felt partly excited thinking this could be an absolutely gorgeous hunk of a man lying next to her as her mind drifts off very quickly thinking about men before her time, "*A man that opens doors, a man that brings flowers!!!*"

Yet Jane was also dumb-struck at the same time wondering whatever possessed her to let a man into her home. Hmm better still, a man into her bed! Back to her thoughts of how this would have occurred, her mind was just... Blank! Completely empty!

With her eyes fixated on a tiny mark on the ceiling, her mind was speculating what her performance had been like the night prior, "*Was I behaved? Was I silly? Was I good in bed? Such a pity I remember bugger all.*"

She kept her breathing slow and steady so she didn't disturb whoever this man was that owned this amazingly scrumptious leg! Trying to pace her steps from leaving her house, to what bar she went in, to what she drank and how much she drank, unfortunately made no difference, Jane was seriously hung over!

Her eyes glanced around the room for clues. She could see her red bra hanging off the purple lampshade. A pair of men's black trousers dangling over the back of the wooden chair. Her red shoe-string top twisted in the window blinds. Her white skirt on the floor and her white knickers hanging off the door handle.

"*Oh Shit!*" she thought, "*Just how many bloody drinks did I actually fucking have last night?*"

This is not like Jane. Jane never goes this far with inviting any man into her home. Her home was her oyster. Man free, stress free and everything just as she likes it. Everything inside her home had a place that no one would ever dare alter. That would completely ruin her day.

On the outside appearance of Jane, she is well dressed with thought and great expense. Well spoken, thoughtful, pleasant, with a bubbly personality. Which to her friends actually gets way better once she has had a few drinks. She becomes more loud, more daring and slutty, not to mention, predictable!

As she started to create a plan of how to escape out of the bed, this man gave a grunt and began shuffling into a different position. His thigh released from hers as he turned on his side facing her, his head immersed under the covers. "*YES!*" Jane thought, "*I can silently slip out of the bed!*"

Instead his arm flopped right across her chest, "*SHIT!*" She laid very very still with shallow breathing so he could not feel her chest moving with each and every breath she took.

She slowly turned her head towards him to try and get a glimpse of who this body belonged to, but the quilt was in the way of his face. "*Dammit!*" She thought.

She laid there thinking real hard... "*Who did I speak to? Did I dance with anyone? Did we kiss? What the fuck happened last night?*" Minute after minute was passing... "*Shit! I need a piss.*" she thought.

She glanced at the bedroom door wondering how on earth her knickers landed on the doorknob and how her top had got tangled up in the window blinds, "*Did we do a stripping game? Were we desperate to get into bed?*" She glimpsed at the clock on the nightstand, it read 7:30 am. Beside the clock were 3 empty condom packets.

Her whole world paused, "*Hmm... if we used 3 and I didn't go to the bathroom, where are they?*" Jane tried to wiggle her toes under the cover to see if she could feel anything inside the bed. She then slowly bent her legs at the knees so her feet were flat on the sheet. She slowly fumbled her feet around her side to see if she could- "*Found one! Uh Oh!*" Jane's big toe had slipped into the opening of the condom, "*Oh Bollocks!!*"

Jane's toe was caught, she didn't know what to do. She tried flicking her big toe in the hope to toss it off, but the more she tried to flick it, the further her toe was going in. She pulled her foot slowly closer to her body so her left hand could reach her toe. She grabbed the condom and flicked it out of the bed which slapped up against the wall before hitting the floor. "*Eww...*" she thought. She gagged and remembered there were still two more to find. Jane did more shallow breathing and attempted to fumble her feet around to find the next one. She moved her feet to the right, to the left, to the right again, even tried circling motions but nope! "*Where the crap are they?*"

Poor Jane... There is a strange man in her bed, although he could be adorable. Two lost condoms. An extremely full bladder while still feeling slightly pissed up from the previous night.

Jane does not seem to have much luck remembering anything after a few drinks or five or seven. She had an idea! She would very gently and very slightly lift his arm off her chest and try a slight side shuffle towards the edge of the bed, "*Here we go…*" she thought.. After counting to three in her head she proceeded to make her first move.

She raised his arm slightly so his skin was not touching hers and gently shuffled her butt to the left followed by her legs then upper body, paused ... and rested his arm on her chest. Success!!! but she realized she had only moved a blip of an inch. Here she goes again...

Raises his arm slightly, shuffles butt to the left followed by the rest of her body and replaces the arm. This took quite a few attempts and took quite a few minutes, that felt like an ongoing rehearsed act inside her head with her inner voice narrating every move she needed to make. Lift arm, shuffle my butt to the left, shuffle legs, shuffle my back and replace arm. "*Shit, this is exhausting!*"

Obviously by now, his arm was no longer reaching completely across her chest. He would surely soon notice the fact that his arm was no longer parallel to her body nor in a comfortable position. But in fact dipped between them like a collapsed bridge.

Jane took note to see how close her body was to the edge of the bed. His hand was only just meeting with the middle of her chest, elbow dipped between them, and she could see she still had about 4 inches to go! "*I've got this!*" Jane told herself, "*Just a little more to go then I can sneak to the bathroom.*" Jane started her played-out moves again...

Lift arm, shuffle butt, shuffle legs, shuffle back, return hand to skin. Lift arm, shuffle butt, shuffle legs, shuffle back, hand... to this deep voice saying ... "Morning gorgeous!"....

In utter silence her lips mouthing the word "*Fuuuuuuuuuuck!!!*" as he stretched his arm across her stomach, hooked his hand underneath her waist and pulled her close to him, causing Jane to flip on her side with her back to him and cradled by his embrace that was so flippin tight she was absolutely sure her bladder was going to explode at any given moment. She felt his breath on the back of her neck while he did intermittent, "Mmmm's" while sniffing her neck and her hair.

   Jane didn't know what to do. She was stuck in his embrace, close to an exploding bladder and needing a very very good plan to release herself. Jane and this man's bodies are spooning each other in the middle of the bed, with his head resting on his pillow, while Jane's head was on the bed in-between both pillows facing her pillow. As her arm stretched towards the underneath of her pillow she felt something, something that felt greasy! "*Oh shit! NO NO NO NO!!! Oh bollocks it is!*" Yep!!! There lay condom number two underneath Jane's pillow, greasy and completely utterly used!

   As much as Jane was realizing she must have had a whale of a time in bed last night, still nothing comes to mind. She didn't even know the name of the man lying directly behind her. Was this an embarrassment for Jane? Nope, not a chance. Jane is accustomed to piss ups every weekend and landing a kiss on someone by the end of the night. To actually have a man in her bed? Not accustomed to as Jane would normally be on the back seat of a car or up against a wall in a bar toilet.

This time must have been different as to why Jane invited this man to her bedroom. Who knows, even Jane doesn't know.

Let's briefly give a heads-up of Jane. Jane is not an alcoholic, but Jane will drink pints, shots, shorts and eat jellies. Basically anything that has even a sniff of alcohol, it will end up going down Jane's fucking throat! Why? Because Jane likes to get so pissed up that her brain will automatically push any event deep into her unconscious mind with the result of never being able to tell the tale.

As one would put it, Jane is without a doubt the life of the party. Just don't ask her what happened as she simply cannot tell you and has to rely on everyone else to put the pieces together.

Jane's bladder was calling out for relief. The discomfort was setting in. She needed the bathroom and she needed it now! She gave a grunt as if half asleep and wiggled onto her front to release her from this man. His arm was gently laying across her back. Thankfully he was fast asleep again.

Jane relaxed, shuffled away from him towards the edge of the bed and was in the best position to escape and head to the bathroom. She slowly moved onto her side and was just about to roll off the bed to the floor when he let out this almighty fart. Jane froze, mouth open in a gasp trying not to giggle loudly. The smell started to radiate from under the cover, seeping through the opening at the top. The smell was like rotten eggs mixed in with beer. She turned her head away from the bed sheet in desperation to find clean air. The man gave a grunt and rolled over facing the other way.

Jane, still trying to breathe and trying hard not to laugh out loud, was slowly compelling herself to regain focusing on the bathroom that she so desperately needed to relieve her nearly exploding bladder.

"*Ok, so he is now facing the other way, I am close to the edge of the bed. All I need to do is to roll off onto the floor but quietly!*" Jane was getting ready for her final move...

"*After the count of three... One, two, three!!!*"

She rolled out of the bed but her head hit the nightstand, which caused a loud bang. Her body flopped onto the floor as if she had no bones in her body. That disturbed the man in the bed. He shuffled back facing her side saying, "Oh babe are you alright? What did you do? Come have a cuddle."

Jane instantly pulled herself back onto the bed, laid on her side with her back to him with one hand holding her head "Oooh bugger arghhhh, oooh fuck that hurt arghhh." With a sleepy attempt with his hand flopping in-between, he attempted to stroke her head to soothe her... "There there, there there." he said, "Stay with me babe."

Jane cringes every time she hears any man say the word babe! She absolutely hates that word and the word always comes with a sound as if the person is suffering with blocked sinuses.

It's like that moment you hear, "Alright babe!" Your eyes close and you feel yourself forcing that vomit feeling right back down to the pit of your gut. Poor Jane, all she wants is to get the fuck out of bed, go for a piss and try and remember how she got herself bogged down with a man in her bed to which she currently still does not know his name or how the hell he got here.

As his body pressed up tight against hers and his arm once again flops over her, Jane feels his breath as he again starts sniffing her hair in-between breaths and mutters, "You're gorgeous babe!"

"*WTF*" Jane thinks, "*why does he keep sniffing my fucking hair?*" A paused moment of thought, then it clicks... Jane had used a rare find of shampoo called 'Love In The Making'. She had bought it from a peddler at a stall at the market last week and now remembers the peddler winking at her as she handed over the cash to pay for it. She instantly remembers talking with the peddler.

"Love In The Making huh? I don't think even this will bring me the man of my dreams."

"You use," the peddler said, "You find your desires."

Jane had just looked at him as if he had totally lost the plot.

"Chance would be a fine thing." Jane replied.

The peddler was standing there smiling at her with his eyes squinted the whole time until she paid. As she walked away holding her apparently desire-fulfilling shampoo the peddler was grinning and nodding as if he had just sent her on a lustful conquest. Jane never thought to read what was in the shampoo, she just left it in her bathroom until last night being the first time of using it.

She was deep in thought about the shampoo and the peddler when she suddenly felt these pelvic grinding motions against her butt cheeks. Her eyes rolled and deep down inside she sighed, *"How am I ever going to get out of this bed?"* Jane thought.

"You like that babe? Mmmm babe you smell so good! I want you babe!"

Jane didn't know how to respond and instead, a little giggle came out. *"OMG I just giggled!"* She thought...

"You know, this could be the man of my dreams lying next to me, he could also be my worst nightmare. He could be really hunky like the men in those magazines OR he could be

rough looking with wiry hair, and spotty or have buck teeth. Does he have long hair? Or short hair? Is he clean-shaven? Does he have a neat stubble or does he just look like he hasn't shaved or washed in weeks? Normal, he could be normal, does normal exist? What is normal? Is it a man that sits with a newspaper? Is it a man that likes to party? Oh! Does a normal man want endless kids? Or maybe just one? Maybe a normal man wants one kid AND likes to party, now that would be a win win!" Thoughts are just streaming through Jane's mind trying to picture a normal, hunky, party going type of man. "*OMG! What is that!!!*"

The normal was broken... Jane could not believe what she was feeling right now. She felt this sudden hardness pressing up against her.

"*Oh no no no! Oh no no no! This is not happening!*"

But yes, it was happening…

"Mmmm babe! Mmmm Babe!" his voice was getting deeper and deeper. His pelvis grinding with his throbbing member poking her butt cheeks! Jane lies there completely stunned feeling this motion of the grind.

"*Are you fucking kidding me!!!*"
His grinding turns into a pelvic thrust with the intermittent poke, poke, poke, poke.

"*This has to stop! I can't fucking do this!*"
Jane started to do a random cough in the hope that his full on hardness will just deflate and crawl back into its shell instead of hitting her in the butt cheek.

"Cough… Cough… … Cough…"
"*It's not working!!!*"
"Cough! Cough!! Cough!!!"
Jane is panicking, she needs a much better plan. His arm clutches across her chest tightly with every pelvic thrust he makes. His face is buried in the back of her hair and his heavy morning breath is oozing down the back of her neck. His deep voice vocalizes, "Stay with me babe…"

Jane lets out a sudden, "Fuck me!!"
"YES!!!" he says.
As Jane leaps out of bed, she slips on the condom and falls flat on her arse.
"Where are you going babe?"
She scrambles to pick herself up. Grabs her knickers off the door handle, steps into them

while running down the hallway with her boobs flapping left to right while fighting gravity as Jane frantically heads for the bathroom door.

Chapter two

The Bathroom Chaos

As Jane bursts through the bathroom door she scuffles around quickly to close the door and lock it behind her. She stood out of breath leaning forward with her hands evenly spread against the door panting. Her head hanging low with her back arched forwards, "Oh blimey!" She whispers to herself.

Jane is happy she finally escaped the bed. As her breathing became calm she lifted her head, released her hands from the door and took a few steps back and parked her knickered covered arse on the edge of the bath with her hands clutching the bath either side of her body.

She looked down at her naked tummy seeing the few ripples from slouching across her middle "*Ooof...*" Jane straightened her back, looked up to the ceiling and sighed again, "*Oh shit! I needed a piss!*"

She shuffled towards the toilet, pulled down her knickers, parked her arse onto the toilet and slouched. Elbows on her knees with her head resting into her hands. "*What a night!, what a morning!*"

Jane had to know what happened the night before. While she was pissing for England she started thinking about what friends she could message and realized, yep! Jane had left her phone and her clothes in the bedroom. "*Well shit! I'm going to have to go get them...*"

She wiped herself and pulled up last night's knickers and thought about how she was going to get back in the bedroom unnoticed.

"*Ok here we go...*" She slowly and quietly unlocked the bathroom door ... CLICK!!! Went the lock, "Oh shit!" She muttered. She edged the door open, paused to listen to the silence then made her move.

She tip-toed through the hallway until she was close to the bedroom doorway. Slapped her back up against the wall then slid down the wall to a crouch then to her hands and knees and crawled through the bedroom doorway. As she crawled in she lifted her head slightly to look at the bed… Just a huge hump of covers with no man in view. She crawled some more around the end of the bed… Poked her head up again to take another peek.

As she got to her dresser she slowly reached her arm up to the top drawer and slightly opened it and pulled out a fresh pair of black lacy knickers. She reached into the drawer again and pulled out a white bra. She then reached for the second drawer, opened it slightly and pulled out a white shoestring top. Opened the bottom drawer and pulled out a black frilly mini skirt. Jane flipped the clothes onto her back like a donkey traveling with goods. She backed up then did a three-point turn and crawled on all fours back around the bed peeking her head up on and off to make sure she was not disturbing the possible man of her dreams.

As Jane crawled towards the doorway she remembered her phone was on the bedside table. She backed up in reverse, then forward towards her side of the bed and grabbed her phone and placed the end of the phone between her teeth. Then while on all fours backed the fuck out of the bedroom in full speed, tits intermitantly slapping her in the neck. Jane reversed all the way out into the hallway before getting on her feet, grabbed her clothes and re-entered the bathroom again locking the door behind her.

She put her clean clothes on top of the towel rack and her phone on the toilet seat. She stood in front of the mirror and just stared at her thick curly ginger hair with auburn highlights that were frizzy so bad it looked like she had been pulled through a hedge backwards. She just stared at her reflection, "Oh blimey, look at me!" she told the mirror.

Her eyeliner was smudged under her eyes. Her skin looked like it had never seen an ounce of water. Remains of her makeup were all blotchy and she looked like she was severely lacking in sleep. Her eyes looked tired and she had a banging headache. She straightened her back, took a long hard look at herself and decided... "*Yep that was a fucking good night, I think?*" And winked at her reflection. "*A bath, that's what I need.*"

Jane leaned over the bath, placed the plug in, turned on the taps and added a few drops of tropical bubble bath. While the bath was filling up, steam was filling the room making it almost impossible to see herself in the mirror. She gave the mirror a wipe with her hand and stood there staring at the mess of herself. She wiped again then tried to run her fingers through her hair but something didn't feel right.

One side of her hair was a matted lump that was hardish and stuck together like glue. She tried pulling at her hair to separate the mass. She wiped the mirror once more and moved her face closer to try and see what it was. "*OMG!!! NO WAY!*" Yep Jane had found condom number three! "*That is so grose, how the fuck did it get in my hair?*" No matter how much Jane could ask herself this, there would never be a good explanation.

Jane dropped last night's knickers to the floor, stepped out of them and stepped into the bath. Laid back and thought about who she could message.

"*Dammit.*" Her phone was on the toilet seat! Up she got, stepped out and skidded on her wet feet to the toilet seat, "*Oh jeez, that was scary!*" She tiptoed back to the bath being very careful and placed her arse back inside.

She laid back under the bubbles, turned on her phone and scrolled down to find Jazmin.

Jane: *Hiya*
Jazmin: *Hi Hunny!*
Jane: *WTF happened last night?*
Jazmin: *????*
Jane: *You were with me last night right?*
Jazmin: *Yes hun, until you wandered off*
Jane: *We were at the sunrise bar right?*
Jazmin: *Yes hun, are you ok?*
Jane: *Well, I can't really remember much about last night*
Jazmin: *Oh Jane, you make me laugh, you get yourself into such a state every weekend lol*
Jane: *So were we in the bar all night?*
Jazmin: *Hun, I was in the bar all night but you were not.*
Jane: *I wasn't?*
Jazmin: *No hun, after a few drinks with us you went to another bar with Lizzy.*
Jane: *WHAAAAAAAAAAAAAT????*

Jazmin: *Yes hun, you left us around 8:30 pm.*
Jane: *Us? who is us? Who were we with?*
Jazmin: *LOL, we were with Phil, Eliza, John, Steven and Ebony.*
Jane: *Where the fuck does Lizzy come into this?* Jazmin: *Lizzy came to the bar by herself around 8pm. You seriously do not remember anything?* Jane: *No, I flippin don't!!!*
Jazmin: *Oh hun! you're so funny. Why don't you try messaging Lizzy :) I must go, Phil and I are going for coffee, speak soon xxx*

Jane closed her eyes... "*WTF! Lizzy? I went off with Lizzy? I don't remember seeing Lizzy... I don't remember ANYTHING!!!*"

Jane applied a facial mud mask, laid back and wondered about texting Lizzy. "*If I don't do this now I will never know and I need to know...Do I want to know? I don't know .. Yes! I need to know!!!*"

Jane: *Hey Lizzy*
Lizzy: *OMFG JANE!!!*
Jane: *Ha ha I guess you were expecting a text from me?*
Lizzy: *Why do you ask that?*

Jane: *Apparently I left with you to go to another bar?*
Lizzy: *Erm yeah, but you didn't stay long, Oh my! do you remember ANYTHING from last night? LOL*
Jane: *NOPE!*
Lizzy: *SERIOUSLY?*
Jane: *Why, what did I do?*
Lizzy: *What didn't you do would be the question lol*
Jane: *Oh boy!! All I know is I woke up with a banging headache and a man in my bed!!!*
Lizzy: *WHAAAAAAAAT?*
Lizzy: *WHO IS IT?*
Lizzy: *LOL*
Jane: *Wait, you have no idea who I left the bar with?*
Lizzy: *No sweetie I don't. Who is he?*
Jane: *I have no idea, I haven't looked at his face.*
Lizzy: *You have a fucking man in your bed and you have not looked at his face? What kind of shit is that? lol*
Jane: *Hey I was shit faced last night, I don't remember anything I mean NOTHING!!!*

Lizzy: *Jane, you are the only girl I know that could pull this shit off LOL*
Jane: *Ha ha very funny, so what did I do last night when I was with you?*
Lizzy: *Where do I start LOL, You were drinking with a guy called Fred, then you got up on the table and started dancing and singing Wannabe by the spice girls LOL*
Jane: *Yeah yeah sure!!!!*
Lizzy: *If you wanna be my lover....*
Jane: *OMG STOP!!! What else did I do?*
Lizzy: *You kissed Fred HAHA!!!*
Jane: *WHAT?*
Lizzy: *Yeah, you snogged him, Infact.. You both snogged so much he had dribble on his chin when you stopped LOL, you then went to the toilet and never came back to us lol*
Jane: *NO NO NO I didn't, did I?*
Lizzy: *It was so grose.. yet so flippin epic!!!*
Jane: *Did I leave with him?*
Lizzy: *NO! Fred ended up staying with us.. I have no clue where you went.*
Jane: *UGH!!! What bar were we in?*

Lizzy: *The Tin Hat, I remember seeing Tina last night. She was sitting at the bar near the toilets, try texting her :)*
Jane: *I don't know if I have her number, let me check.*
Jane: *Yep I do.*
Lizzy: *Ok sweetie, have fun and say hi to whoever is in your bed!!! you saucy girl LOL*

"*Damn... wtf... I kissed Fred? Who the fuck is Fred?*"

Jane gave a sigh and laid with her eyes closed until her face started cracking. Jane is just nowhere forward right now, but she could feel her face getting tighter and tighter as the mud mask dried. She made an enormous smile that made the mud mask feel like it broke into a thousand little pieces that broke away and flurried like ashes into the bubbles.

She got up, stepped out of the bath and looked in the mirror. Pulled some more silly faces then grabbed her face cloth and started to remove the remains of the mud pack. She rinsed her face, returned to the bath and wacked up the hot tap to top up the lukewarm water. She laid back and slid her body under the depleting bubbles, "More bubbles needed." Jane said to herself! She added more tropical bubble bath but unfortunately poured way too much under the running hot water without thinking and slid back under the water and closed her eyes.

It wasn't long before the bubbles were multiplying at a rapid rate and eventually making contact with her chin. The bubbles!!! Oh, they were multiplying all right! A foot of bubbles and still multiplying like someone had a bubble machine directly inside the bathtub. The bubbles waited patiently for Jane to come to the surface of the water to turn the tap off!!! "*Ooof, wtf... oh bollocks!!! Too many bubbles!!!*"

As Jane fumbled her way to the tap with a tower of foaming bubbles sky high on her head and dripping off her face. Her arms covered. Her chest just lost in the depths. If anyone saw her they would think she had some form of explosion all over her.

"*FUCK!!!*" Ah yes and there is the famous Jane word... Fuck! "*How the fuck am I going to get washed with all this shit!?*" She grabbed her bar of soap, "*Bubbles don't like soap...*" She over-lathered her arms and her chest in the hope that the bubbles would start to disintegrate, but it was not working out as well as she hoped for. There were far too many!

"*Good grief this is sooooo stuuuupid!*" She stood up to lather her arse, lady parts and legs still living with the hope that the bubbles would just go away. "*Oh bugger off already, get off me! Go away!!!*" The voice in her head, "*Take the plug out and use the shower!*" Jane's mouth, "Oh jeez please just get off me!!!"

As she is still pursuing the 'soap will do it' hack, the bar is getting thinner and thinner with Jane looking like she has thick cream all over her body heightened with endless bubbles that will not do as they are told.

"Dammit, ugh!!" Jane finally gave in, pulled the plug out of the bath, reached for the shower head, and started to wash her concoction towards the plug hole. So she thought! There were so many bubbles they were reaching up to her knees so Jane started spraying them down inside the bathtub.

"*Flip this isn't working!*" Maybe if Jane used cooler water the bubbles would start to diminish! She reached for the hand towel and threw it on the floor and raised her first leg up, showered off the bubbles then placed her foot out and onto the towel. She then did her other leg.

"Wahoo!!! I'm finally out of the bloody bath!" Yet the amount of bubbles still left inside was no laughing joke. She switched the water to cold, placed the shower head inside the bath under the masses and left it there to do its job of eliminating her own well-made mess while she dried herself. She grabbed her large towel, swung it around her shoulders and gathered it up, enclosing her into a cocoon with the corner notched in to hold it in place.

She grabbed her shampoo which was not the one from the pedler, this was actual shampoo for ginger hair. I guess this shampoo had an added ingredient to soften the wiry look. She turned on the basin taps and shoved her head in this small space and finally washed out all the bubbles from the bath and the matted clump caused by the leaking condom she found.

She twisted her wet hair into another towel then attended to the bath. "*Oh here we go!*" She picked up the shower head, sat her arse on the edge of the bath and directed the flow of water pushing the bubbles towards the plug hole. When Jane was finally done, she hung the shower head back up and continued to get herself ready.

She opened her makeup case and started the process of smothering her face with a covering of foundation. She worked it in making sure no one could see she had been up to shenanigans the night prior. She needed to look fresh, awake and completely innocent. She then applied the face powder, blusher, eye shadow, lipstick then finally the eyeliner. Misting her face with water to secure the makeup, she did not want any to wear off during the entire day.

Now her hair… She pulled the towel off her hair to reveal this ginger bird's nest that she needed to do something with. She ran a wide-toothed comb through and began with the hair dryer blasting her hair at great speed. She decided to leave her hair down today. Jane's hair was bra strap length at the back, nice even waves with her hair running down each side of her face just past the shoulders. Until it was dry!

As she gave her hair another fast blast her hair was shrinking in length and yep... Those nice even waves turned into curls that brought her hair right up to her shoulders. Her hair poofed out either side, her fringe became level with her jawline. She stuck a pink bow on one side of her hair... I have no idea why, but we are talking about Jane right?

Jane dropped the towel and got dressed in the clothes she had masterfully collected from the bedroom on her hands and knees. Sprayed herself with a fruity smelling perfume then glanced at the mess she had made in the bathroom. She put the towels in the wash basket, her makeup case away, the shampoo back and rinsed her lost strands of hair out of the basin.

Now, what was Jane's next move going to be? She cannot stay in the bathroom all day, she would have to face the music soon to see who was in her bed. Or did Jane have other plans? Of course she did!

Chapter three

Latte & Vodka

Jane stood still, staring at the bathroom door. She grabbed her phone off the toilet seat, took a deep breath and slowly unlocked the door. As she slowly opened the door she listened for any noises coming from the bedroom. There was nothing, she could have heard a pin drop! Just total silence.

She tiptoed out of the bathroom and into the kitchen and poured herself a glass of water from the dispenser. She placed the empty glass ever so gently into the sink avoiding any noise. She tiptoed into the living room, grabbed her handbag and placed her phone inside then headed for the front door. She squeezed her feet into her black stilettos making her 2.5 inches taller than her original 4 ft 5 height.

She slowly unlocked the front door and quietly opened it just enough for her to slither her body out and very gingerly pulled the door shut. As she stepped down the 3 steps outside her front door she took a deep sigh of relief that she was finally out of the house.

"Holy shit! I seriously need a coffee!"

Jane headed down the road strutting her stuff past shops gazing at herself in the large shop windows, nodding to herself in satisfaction with the clothes she had picked out for today. With her hair bouncing upon every step she took and her frilly mini skirt flapping in the breeze her eyes could see her favourite famous coffee shop ahead.

'Titania's Cafe' is the place to be. Set on one of the busiest streets of the city pulling in all walks of life. Extremely good coffee, high service and a good atmosphere. This cafe has also been known to have seen the occasional celebrity pass through. Fancy tables outside with parasols. Fancy tables inside, racks of freshly made bread. Fresh cakes with refreshing salads for a luxurious brunch. You pay the price for the indulgence of endless different types of coffee and food.

"Right! time for a rip roaring latte!" Jane struts in and makes her way to the counter.

"Good morning ma'am, how may I help you?"

"I would like a large latte with extra cream, chocolate shavings and a straw please."

"Anything else?"

"Oh yes! I would also like the strawberry shortcake please."

"Certainly Ma'am. Your total comes to £37.95."

Jane swipes her card.

"Ma'am, take yourself to your favourite table and we will bring your order to you."

"Thank you, I will take the table outside on the right."

Jane points to the table with the purple parasol and struts over to her chosen table. She takes a seat and pulls out her phone ready to text Tina.

"Your latte and shortcake ma'am."

"Thank you!"

Now… This strawberry shortcake is just unbelievable. White biscuit base with fresh strawberries mixed in with a light and fluffy cheesecake filling. A top layer of light sponge topped with fresh cream, with 4 halves of fresh strawberries down the center. This was huge and just divine.

Jane uses the fork to put a huge chunk in her mouth, swipes her phone and begins texting in search for answers.

Jane: *Hi Tina, I need to talk with you.*
Tine: *Okaaaay what's up?*
Jane: *Last night, you saw me leave the Tin Hat?*
Tina: *I saw you do lots of things last night.*
Jane: *Yeah yeah I have already heard, I'm trying to find out when I left and who I left with.*
Tina: *Ahhh, well, after you finished flaunting yourself across tables and snogging Fred, I think you left around 9:30 pm.*
Jane: *Do you know Fred?*
Tina: *I sure do*
Jane: *How?*
Tina: *He works in the bakers where we get our supplies from.*
Jane: *Oh! erm, well ... I don't think I have ever seen him before.*
Tina: *Of course you wouldn't remember seeing him before, you're always pissed up.*
Jane: *Hmm I guess ... anyway, did I leave with anyone?*

Tina: *Jane, you left with Sadie and Pete.*
Jane: *Sadie? Pete? Who the fuck are they?*
Tina: *OMG Jane, you met them in the bar last night.*
Jane: *I don't remember :(*
Tina: *Jane, get your shit together! You went to the toilets, came out, offered them a drink at the bar, then you all left together around 9:30 pm.* Jane: *WTF! You know where we were going?* Tina: *No Jane I don't, good luck with tracing your steps, I have to get back to work, cya later*

Jane paid attention to her strawberry shortcake, mouthful after mouthful of this divine taste until the whole lot had been devoured. By now, her latte was cool enough to drink through the straw. When she reached the bottom of the tall glass she took the straw out and slid her tongue all the way down the straw and back up the other side, making sure to not miss any cream or chocolate for that matter. The latte was so good Jane was thinking about having another one, after all this chapter is called Latte! She approached the counter and requested a refill on her expensive drink.

"Your total is £18.00."

"Thank you!"

"We will bring it over to you once it is ready."

Jane took herself back to her seat. Her drink was brought over but missing the straw. Jane forgets where she is and puts her hand up in the air shouting out, "Oi! Can I have a straw?"

"Yes ma'am!"

"Oh my goodness!" (posh voice back in place), "I am so sorry, I was lost in a moment, I do hope you can forgive my moment of bad manners."

"No problem ma'am."

Jane looks around, "*Thank fuck there was only two older people at another table.*" Thankfully for Jane they didn't even look up from their coffee.

Jane didn't know what to do. She had no number for Sadie, nor Pete. Assuming they were both together in a relationship. She really didn't want to go back into the Sunrise Bar or the Tin Hat at this point. Not until she knew more about her night out.

She decided once she had finished her 2nd latte, she would go into a different bar. An afternoon drink wouldn't hurt and had a very slim chance of bumping into anyone from last night. She stood up, flung her bag over her shoulder and left Titania's Cafe. She walked down the main street until she saw a place she could go into for a quiet drink. Jane… a quiet drink, that has to be a first!

"*Well this place looks alright!*" Jane looked up at the sign 'The Tap'. She pushed the door open, walked in and headed straight for the bar. This was a small bar, ample stools and tables around the outside of the room. Jane hitched herself up onto a bar stool and waited to be served.

"Hi there, what can I get for you?"

"Erm, vodka and orange please with ice."

"Coming right up!"

Jane's eyes looked around the room to make sure she didn't know anyone in the bar.

"There you go, that will be £6.50."

Jane paid for her drink and took a sip.

A man on another bar stool looked over and smiled at Jane. Jane did a half smile back while her brain started to go into overdrive. "*Oh shit! Does he know me? Did he see me last night?*

DID I SNOG HIM TOO!!!? Oh stop it!" she told herself. There is absolutely no way she would've been in this bar last night. Or was she?

The man on the other bar stool just kept staring and smiling at her. He was slightly tubby, hunched shoulders, dark hair with a receding line and a needed trim on his overgrown stubble.

"Hi, my name is Dan. What is your name?"

Oh wow how creepy does that sound, she thought. "I'm Jane." she said and gave a slight nod confirming her own name.

"Nice to meet you Jane."

She gave another nod with a slight smile then looked down at her nearly empty glass.

"Refill miss?"

"Yes please."

"Let me buy that for you." said the creepy man.

"Oh thank you but I got this."

The bartender placed her glass on the bar, "£6.50 miss."

"Thank you."

As Jane was drinking her refill she could feel her tummy start to gurgle. I guess two chocolate lattes and vodka & orange really do not mix very well.

"Are you ok Jane?"

"Yes Dan, I am fine." She wasn't fine... her stomach was starting to gripe. She knew she would have to run to the bathroom very soon.

"What do you have planned for today Jane? Anything exciting?" Oh this Dan was not going to leave her alone!

"Erm, things!"

She couldn't concentrate, the gripes were getting worse, she could feel a fart brewing up...

"Would you like another drink?"

"Sorry Dan, I will be right back!"

Jane grabbed her bag and her drink and ran to the ladies room. Who does this!!! We will keep a closed door on that one, OR not!!!

The cramps, the farts, the water, the smell!!! If you are wanting any more defined details, may I suggest, two chocolate lattes with extra cream and a vodka and orange fifteen minutes later. Let's just assume that Jane did not have a great experience, but had instant relief which gave more room for more drink and food.

As Jane emerged from the Ladies room, she took a quick peep around making sure no other females were in the bar to give time for the awful smell she left behind to vanish. That would be very embarrassing, even for Jane. She does have standards, just not very high ones.

She made her way back to the bar and... "*O-M-G, that Dan is still there, but HELLO!!! Who was he talking to?*" Jane saw this tall dark haired slim man sitting next to Dan. Does this mean Jane will approach? Oh, absobloodylutely!

"Sorry about rushing off Dan, I had to make a quick phone call."

"That's okay Jane, would you like a drink now?"

"Sure Dan."

"Want a pint Mike?"

"Sure."

"Oh, so this is Mike? Hi Mike, nice to meet you."

"Hi Jane, what brings you to this bar?"

"Oh, I thought I would have a nice quiet afternoon drink."

"In this bar? Quiet? Haha!"

"Well, it has been pretty quiet so far."

"That's because everyone was pissed up last night. They probably all woke up with a hangover. Get them often yourself Jane?"

Jane just stared at him wondering if he knew something, or saw something last night.

"Hmm. Haha Mike!"

Mike spun his seat round and took a hard look at Jane then faced the bar again. Watch out, Jane's brain has awoken! "*Oh holy shit! This man is fucking gorgeous!!! What I wouldn't do with this man! Ok keep your cool, take it slow. Oh boy, this is hard, casual conversation is needed!*"

"So Dan, what do you do for work?"

"I'm in construction."

"Nice nice, what about you Mike?"

"I am a DJ in a local bar."

"Hmmm, you can build up my beat anytime!"

"What?"

"Nothing nothing, oh look... My drink!" Jane stammered, "So Mike... What bar do you DJ in?"

"The old Smokey Bar."

"Oh, I am not sure if I have been in that one before."

"You might have!" He winked at Jane.

Jane stopped talking and just dived into her drink. Yet her mind didn't stop talking to her, "*WTF was that supposed to mean? Did I go in there last night? So far, three friends have not shed much light on last night, definately no mention of 'The old Smokey Bar'*"

"So Jane, what do you do for work?"

"Well Dan, glad you asked. I actually work in designing for conventions."

"Oh nice! Any places you have done around here?"

"Yes, I have set up the Plaza a few times and the Rumble House, but most of my work is further away in other cities."

"I bet that pays well Jane."

"It does indeed Dan, it does indeed…"

"Be right back Dan, need a leak."

"Sure thing Mike!"

"Dan... what's the deal with grumpy Mike?"

"Oh I don't know, he gets like that sometimes."

"I see, I see."

"Welcome back Mike." World record piss by Mike. He must have jet streamed from the door, "But I do need to go, I have important things to do. Was nice meeting you Dan. Nice to meet you Mike, hope you learn how to smile more often."

"Are you kidding me?"

"Just kidding Mike! See ya, thanks for the drink Dan!"

Jane left the bar, made her way down the street and thought about what her next bar will be. That was Jane's important thing to do... To search for another bar that had nothing to do with last night. Does Jane even remember there is a man lying in her bed? Does she have any intentions to go back to her home today? She needs to understand that she simply cannot stay out all day denying the body under her sheets. She needs to face the music at some point and she could be missing out. This could be the man of her dreams! I'm pretty sure right now, she is steering clear for as long as possible.

"*No more lattes for me today! I need a good wake up drink! Hmm and some food. I am so flippin hungry right now. OK, food then a good wake up drink!!! Ooh look at this place, 'Brunch A La Carte' let's take a peek in here shall we?*"

Chapter four

The Cocktail Bar

This place looked very charming, sophisticated... Is this a place for our Jane? The tables were laid in a very posh manner. People were dressed in dresses and suits, and here is our Jane in her frilly skirt and high heels. "*Oh my! I feel a little out of place here.*" She straightened her shoulders, tried to ruffle her skirt a little lower to try and hide a section of her thighs and sat at an empty table.

A posh voice behind her said, "Good afternoon madam, and how may we possibly help you?"

WOW, rude!!! Jane tried putting her own posh voice on, "Well hello there, I would like a sandwich please."

"A what?"

"A sandwich! You heard me!"

"I am sorry, we do not make sandwiches here."

"Oh really? Then what is that lady eating? Let me ask again. May I have a hammy slapped in bready with a little lettuce and cuuuuucumber?"

The waiter scowled at Jane, but Jane just scowled right back at him.

"I think you should find a place more suitable to you."

"Hey, I think you're right! This place sucks balls!"

Jane got up from the table tilted her head upwards and strutted, yes strutted her arse right out of there. I didn't think this was a place for Jane. "*Now what! Gonna have to find another place now.*" She walked round the corner to see this extremely lit up sign, 'Shaker & Slice', "*Well this looks more like me.*"

As Jane entered the bar, she saw the entire inside just lit up with pretty lights. A glowing wood fire on one side with cozy couches with side tables, a real snug place. The other side was a bar with music, a few slot machines, tables and chairs. Also pretty lights behind the bar with a line up of mixers and bottles, "*Oh I like this, and look at the lineup of all those bottles behind the bar, how yum! This is going to be a fun time."*

She hitched her frilly skirt back up revealing her thighs and walked slowly through the people nodding her head at them in agreement as the ladies were wearing similar clothes to hers, *"Oh yes, I am in the right place for sure!"* Jane approached the bar.

"What will It be miss?"

"Hmm let me see... Oh, I will have a large vodka to start with."

"Sorry miss, you have to have 2 or more drinks in one glass."

"Oooh I like the sound of that! Stick a tequila in there too!"

The bartender looked shocked at her mix, shrugged his shoulders and prepared her drink.

"There you go miss, that will be £13.00."

Jane hands the money over and takes a good sip of her drink through the straw…

"OH BLIMEY that hits hard!" Her eyes widened like someone had stuck matches in her eyes. Her mouth was open in shock as the drink hit the back of her throat.

"You ok miss? Is your drink too strong for you?"

"Never! Just wasn't expecting it to hit harder than a dick in the back of my throat!"

The bartender gasped at Jane while she just stuck the straw back in her mouth. Eyes strongly fixed on him and sucked away through her straw.

"*OOH That was good! That was the wake up drink I needed!*"

"HEY! Bartender! I will take another one of those please and some… Oooh nuts on the bar! Nevermind I will eat these nuts for now!"

"Your drink miss, £13.00."

"Thank you Mr. bartender."

Jane, clutching her glass, swung round on her bar stool to look around, to see what everyone else was up to and of course to see if there is anyone that she would recognize from last night! Others were in their little groups giggling amongst themselves. A man walked up to the bar and stood next to Jane.

"Well hello there, what is your name?, you good looking sir?"

"Haha, hello back to you, my name is Keith."

Jane slapped him on the shoulder while giggling.

"So what is your name miss?"

"I am Jane."

"Well hello Jane, would you like a drink?"

"Oh sure, that will be a large vodka and a tequila!"

"That's an interesting drink! I will have the same. Two of what Jane is drinking please."

"Coming right up!" Replied the Bartender.

"Sweet, you're gonna love it, it hits the back of your throat like a d…"

"Your drinks sir, £26.00."

"You were saying Jane?"

"Oh erm ... nothing, just thinking out loud, how is your drink?"

"It is actually very nice, very potent but nice."

"I knew you would love it, it has that certain punch in the back of your throat!"

"It does."

"KEITH!!! How ya doing?"

"Alright Steve, how are you?"

"Good good, what are you drinking?"

"Well, I am trying out Jane's drink, Jane, this is my mate Steve."

"Hi Steve!"

"Hi Jane, nice to meet you. So what is this drink?"

"I will order a round for you to try. Keith, my round, my round... Bar tender? three of my drinks this time."

"Coming right up, miss."

"Get ready for the punch in the throat lads!"

"Oh wow, you weren't kidding! This is actually nice."

"Let's call my drink... 'Throat puncher!"

"Sounds good Jane, haha!"

The bartender is listening to their nonsense, but does just play along.

"Thanks Keith."

"Okay... Jane and Keith, are you ready for another round?"

"Yes!"

"Absolutely."

"Bartender, three Throat Punchers!"

They all giggled with full blown silliness, enough to make the bar tender squirm.

"Hey you two lovely lads, let's pool our money on the counter for Mr bartender!"

"Good idea." replied Keith.

"Hey, let's try a different drink next. What should we mix?"

"Good idea Steve, how about Spiced rum and..."

"TEQUILA!!!!!!"

"Funny Jane... but we could try that!"

"Oooh yeah, let's call it… 'The Boom Shaker!"

"Keith, you heard the lady... Three Boom Shakers!!!"

"Hey bartender, over here mate! Three Boom Shakers!"

"Boom shakers huh? What have you chosen in this?"

"Spiced rum and-"

"TEQUILA!!" came bursting out of Jane's mouth.

"Coming right up."

Bartender takes the money off the bar.

Jane feels a slap across her back...

"Jane? Is that you?"

"OMG Sasha!!! How are you?"

"I'm Great! Let's have a drink!"

"Well ok, but you have to have the Boom Shaker!"

"Sure…"
"Guys, guys, meet my friend Sasha!"
"Hi Sasha!" Keith gave her a welcoming hug.
"Hi Sasha!" Steve nodded.

Keith sticks his fingers in his mouth and lets out a large whistle to get the bartender's attention.

"Four boom shakers please!"
"Coming right up."
"Ok Sasha, try this!"

Jane is again pissed up, getting loud but life is grand!

"Oh my! That is an amazing drink Jane!"
"Sure is, sure is."
"Keith! My round, my round!"
"Sure Steve, you ladies up for another?"
"Absobloodylutely!"
"Sasha?"
"Yes!!!"
"Here you are! We need to think of another drink!"
"Sure Keith, but I need a piss!"

Jane stumbles off the barstool, falls onto Sasha, tries to stand up straight but falls backwards onto Steve.

"You alright Jane?"

"Yup yup Steve... I... am... peachy!"

They all watch Jane swaying and bouncing off everyone in her path to get to the ladies room. As much as Jane is already absolutely pissed as a fart, there is always more room for oodles of drink. Oh watch out, Jane is heading back... Is she going to make it?

"MAKE WAY! MAKE WAY! COMING THROUGH!" Jane's arms are swaying like a zombie telling everyone to get out of her way, "OH Blimey... this song... again!!!"

She climbed onto a table and started flapping her arms about singing from the top of her lungs...

"IF YOU WANNA BE MY LOVER, you got to get with my friends, make it last forever, FRIENDSHIP NEVER ENDS!!!"

"OMG you lot, look at Jane!"

"Incredible Steve." Keith nudges Sasha, "Sasha look, hahaha!"

"Oh not again!!! LOL!"

"Again?" Keith asks.

"Yeah, she did this last night too!"

"I gather this is her regular bar?"

"Nah Keith, every bar is her regular!"

Jane stumbles back over to the bar with a massive grin on her face, "Sorry guys, I love that song, I just had to!"

"That's fine, you were great!!! Here, sit on the stool!"

"Thanks Steve!"

Keith boldly says, "So I hear you did the same thing last night haha, in this bar?"

"Wait, what? Was I in here last night?"

"Yep!"

"WTF Sasha!?"

"What?"

"You saw me?"

"Well der!"

"I don't know what happened last night!"

"I think this whole bar knows what you did last night, haha!"

"Funny, funny, do tell me!"

"Do you remember seeing a bloke called Jordan?"

"NOPE!"

"So you don't remember laying on top of him on the floor?"

"NOPE!"

"So you also don't remember giving him a blowjob in the men's toilets!?"

"NOPE!"

"Oh Jane! I need to enlighten you… Around 10:30 pm last night, you stumbled through the door with your friends Sadie & Pete."

"Actually I only met them last night so not friends but had a drink with them!"

"Jane... As soon as you got to the bar you immediately started eyeing up and smiling at a bloke called Jordan.

"Annnnnnd who is this Jordan?"

"Jordan is a regular in this bar on Friday nights. He is a Dr. and Saturdays are his only day off."

"Ooooooh, a doctor? Way to go me!!!"

"Don't get your hopes up Jane, he is married and kindly told you to sod off!!! LOL!"

"Wow! Rude!!! So what happened next?"

"Well, After you turned away from Jordan, you embarrassed yourself by bumping into Barry and spilling your drink over him!"

"Uh huh, uh huh! Keep going!"

"Barry was like, 'Hey missy! What are you doing!?' You replied while leaning right up to his face and saying…'Making you wet!'"

"WTF Sasha! There is no way I would've said that!"

"Unfortunately you did Jane!"

"Did he like it?"

Sasha stared at Jane, "What do you think? Yes he did. He put his arm around you and ushered you to a table!"

"Annnnnnnnnd?"

"Jane, you did your normal thing."

"What's that?"

"FFS Jane, you sat on his lap, snogged him for a while then went to the bathroom!"

"Well did I go back to him?"

"Nope! When you came out of the bathroom you went to the wrong table, sat in a chair and were chatting with people you didn't even know!"

"Well what happened to Barry?"

"He left the bar."

"So it is not Barry who is lying in my bed…"

"Jane? You have a man in your bed?"

"Uh huh!"

"Who?"

"Well if i knew who he was, I wouldn't be on this fucking conquest to find out what in the actual fuck happened last night!!"

"Oh Jane, I am so sorry! I don't know what to tell you!"

"Well, did I leave the bar? Did I leave with anyone else?"

"Actually yes you did. The two people at the wrong table got very chatty with you and you left around 11:15pm."

"But I don't know who they were."

"Look, in about 10 minutes the bar staff will change over, it will be the ones that were working the shift last night. Maybe you could ask them?"

"Hey Ladies, want to sink another Boom Shaker!?"

"Sure Keith!"

"Hey bartender! 4 Boomshakers please!"

"Coming right up" He took £60.00 off the bar.

"Cheers ladies!"

"Cheers!!"

"Well Steve, Jane, Sasha, it has been nice meeting you but I must leave now, have a good evening!"

"Nice meeting you Keith, thanks for the drinks!"

"You too Jane, nice meeting you Sasha!"

"Actually Jane, Sasha, I need to go too, have a nice evening."

"You too Steve, cya later!"

Jane and Sasha sat at the bar chatting, waiting for the bar staff to change shifts. Jane was extremely hammered again while Sasha was doing just fine!

"So, Jane? Did you seriously leave your home with a man in your bed?"

"Yep!"

"Why?"

"Sasha. Since when have I ever taken a man back to my home? I have no pissing clue what happened, or who he is, I didn't even see his face this morning. I woke up to his thigh in between mine".

"WOW Jane! WTF are you going to do?"

"Keep trying to find out what happened is the only thing I can do."

The bar staff changed shifts. Jane looked at the previous evening bar staff and couldn't remember any of their faces.

"Excuse me? Do you remember me from last night?"

"Sure do ma'am."

"I was wondering if you remember seeing me chatting with people at that table over there last night?"

"Yes…"

"Can you tell me their names?"

The bartender looks at Jane and smirks, getting a kick out of knowing Jane cannot remember sod all. As the bartender slowly pulls a pint, he leans forward towards Jane and says, "Terry and Natasha."

"Do you know how I can contact them?"

"Sure, be here around 11:00 pm!"

"Thank you! I will do that!"

"Well Sasha, I suppose I had better get my pissed up arse home with hoping that man is not in my bed anymore and get myself sorted for later!"

"Ok Jane, good luck with that."

"Spend the rest of the money Sasha!"

They hugged each other and Jane staggered towards the bar door and left.

Chapter Five

Just a Thought!

While Jane was staggering home in her high heels, she couldn't help wondering that if she actually took a look at the man in her bed, all her questions would be answered. That also means she would have to face him. No matter who he was or what he looked like. Taking into account that once Jane is full of booze she seems to not care who she approaches.

As she became closer to her home, the butterflies were scrambling in all directions inside her. She walked up her three steps, put the key in the door and paused... *"He could still be in my bed. He could've left. He could be in my bathroom, or sitting on my sofa waiting for me. What if he is drop dead gorgeous? But, what if he is not! It was just one night, surely he would've left by now. OMG this is so hard!!! My head is all fuzzy. Do I go in? Or do I stay out? Come on, mind start talking to me!!!"*

Come on Jane... Just go in and put us all out of our misery! Everyone reading this just wants to know who he is!!!

"*I know what I'm going to do!*"

Yay for Jane!!! She's made her mind up!!!

"*I think it's time for a new outfit!*"

Oh Jane… Clearly she is not ready to confront this man. Sounds like she is taking the easy way out. Oh Jane, this could all be resolved so quickly. OK, let's continue with what Jane did next... She removed the key from the door, backed up down her steps and continued down her street to the shops.

"*LateeBo's Designers… Well that's new! Let's see what they have in here.*" She pushed on the heavy tinted glass door with all her might that just wouldn't open. She regained her concentration and pushed again and again until the other door opened with a man smiling at her.

"This way ma'am."

Jane straightened her back. Ruffled with her top. Smiled at the man and walked through the door to see the other assistants watching her enter. One of the assistants approached Jane with a smirk.

"Hi there ma'am, I am Jannette, is there something particular you are looking for?"

"Hmmm, maybe a short skirt with a matching top." The other assistants were giggling in the background making this very hard for Jannette to keep a straight face.

"We do not sell that kind of attire here, may I show you some lovely dresses?"

"Sure can Jannette, lead the way!!!"

Jannette took a deep breath and led the way towards the back of the shop.

"Here, this is our most popular floral dress."

Jane screwed her face up like an old lady, "No thank you."

"Hmm, well how about the plain colour dresses, maybe this is best suited for you."

This woman is bloody rude, how dare she assume I'm a plain Jane!!!

"Do you have anything in black?"

"We do ma'am, but they might be a little pricey for you."

"Well, JANNETTE, maybe I can decide that without you assuming with your toffee nose!!!"

"Oh!!! Well, come this way Ma'am!" The other staff giggled again.

Jane re-straightened her skirt and top, looked over her shoulder to the other assistants then stuck her nose right up in the air.

"How is this one for you, it is a lace body fitting with underwire. The dress ends just above the knees."

"Can I try this on?"

"Yes, ma'am, the fitting rooms are just over there."

Jane grabs the dress from Jannette and stomps over to the fitting rooms.

"Oh righty then, let's try this on!"

Jane, with lack of balance steps out of her skirt, falls backwards onto the little bench, "Oof, glad that was there!" She pulls off her top, flings it onto the floor, then steps into the dress, "Cor blimey!!! She ain't joking with the tight fitting."

Jane wiggles her body like a worm while edging the dress further up her body and looks in the long mirror, "I like this!!! Where's the bloody tag... Ahh here it is… HOLY SHIT!!! £1575... For this dress?"

Jane stares in the mirror, turns to see how good her butt looks in it. Sees how nice her tummy was 100% flat with her boobs completely formed like little memory foam mattresses. She cupped her hands over her boobs, squeezing them. *"Nice."* she thought! Then she remembered the price. She wiggled out of the dress, hung it on the hanger, and put her clothes back on. "I'm going to have to take it, I cannot turn this down now, they will think I'm poor…" Jane opens the changing room door to see Jannette waiting outside.

"How was the dress ma'am?"

The other assistants ear dropping at the desk.

"I will take this one, thank you."

"Oh well, good choice ma'am, follow me to the desk."

Jane paid for the dress and proudly headed to the door, the man held the door open so Jane didn't embarrass herself again. She was going to need a new pair of shoes and a new handbag. She glanced across the street, saw a cute looking shop and waltzed across the road without a care in the world.

"Ooooh!!! 'Totties' shoe shop, I think I will take a peek in there!" As Jane opened the door, this girl with bright pink hair rushed towards her, "Well hi there lady, looking for a new pair of shoes?"

"I am indeed, and a handbag!"

"Well you have come to the right place, let's get started... What are you wearing tonight?"

"Here I will show you"
Jane pulled out the dress from her bag and held it up.

"Oh wow! Expensive dress! Let's get you a nice new pair of black stilettos!"

"I would like something with a little sparkle, the ones I have on are just plain."

"Sure thing lady! Have a look at these ones, they are sparkly and the same heel height as the ones you're wearing, if that's what you're comfortable with."

"I am, and these are amazing! Can I try them on?"

"Sure thing lady. Oops, be careful! Been on the 'ol booze have ya?"

"Yeah, can you tell?"

"I'd say, a bit tottery lady."

"How much are they?"
"For you lady, £49.00!"
"Ooh nice! I will take these!"
"Perfect! Let's find a nice bag to match… How about this bag? It's sleek and compact with a nice long strap, just enough room for the essentials."
"I like this, how much is this?"
"£25.00."
"I will take this too!"
"There you are, lady, all set up for your evening, hope you have a good time!"
"Thank you!"

Jane left the store, she still had 5 hours until she planned to conveniently bump into Terry and Natasha to see if they could shed any light on Jane's Friday night. She would also have to think of a place to put on her new clothes, and have no idea what will become of her current clothes she is wearing…

"Nails! I'm gonna get my nails done!"

Jane googled on her phone for the nearest nail salon, she walked up to the window and peered in. She could see 2 rows of seating either side of the room, pictures of brightly coloured dragons on the walls with a Chinese written plaque hanging above an opening towards the back of the shop floor. It was extremely busy there, and the chances of Jane getting a walk-in appointment was looking slim, but Jane had hope, an attitude and a plan. She looked up at the shop sign 'Tranquil Tips'.

"*Interesting name.*" Thought Jane. She entered through the door and approached the lady at reception.

"Hello there, would you like to book an appointment?"

"Actually, I would like to be seen now if I can."

"I am so sorry, we are currently busy right now."

"But I need to be seen now, I have to be out later!"

"I am so sorry, we are currently busy right now, we have a cancellation for tomorrow at 2 pm if you would like."

"You don't understand. Please, I need to be seen now."

"Sorry lady, I cannot help you today."

Jane made her bottom lip start to quiver, and produced this weird not crying, but start of crying sound. Making her shoulders move up and down in a frenzy. One of the beauticians came to see what was going on...

"What is your name, lady?"

"Jane, (Sniffles) my name is Jane."

"Jane, what are you needing today?"

"My nails done, I need them pretty for tonight."

"Can you go home and come back in an hour?"

"No!!! I cannot go home!"

"Ok Ok! Take a seat over there and I will see what I can do."

"Oh thank you, thank you, thank you."

Jane put on a huge smile, sniffles evaporated as she took a seat in the waiting area. As she sat there, her eyes noticed all the little red lanterns hanging from the ceiling. *Cute!* She thought.

"Jane come this way please." Jane grabbed her clothes and shoe bags and headed to the nail chair, she stuffed the bags firmly under the seat.

"My name is Lin, I will be your nail technician today."

"You are very pretty Lin."
"Thank you Jane!"
"Your hair is lush!"
"Thank you. Let's neaten these nails for you."

Lin picked up the clippers and began trimming the edges of her nails. Jane rested her head back in the chair. Maybe I could nap!

"Sooo, what have you been up to today?"

Or not!

"Not much."

Lin's eyes looked up towards Jane...

"Have you had a good day?"

"It's been ok."

Lin's eyes looked up towards Jane again.

"You have a man in your life?"

"What? Nooo!"

Lin's eyes looked up at Jane again…

"I am going to glue on the tips now."

"So how are you Lin?"

"Oh I am very good thank you."

"Been a busy day?"

"Always busy days girl!"

Lin coated the first nail with the gel...

"Place thumb under UV light please, hold still."

She coated the next nail...

"Place finger under UV light, hold still. Did you have a good night out last night?"

"Oh erm... I did, actually."

"Where did you go? Place your finger under UV light, hold still."

"In a few bars, I don't actually remember."

"Must've been a good time. Place your finger under UV light and hold still."

"From what I have heard it was a good time."

"And place your finger under UV light, hold still."

Each time Lin's eyes locked in with Janes.

"Ok, let's do your other hand... What are you up to tonight then?"

"What's with all the questions?"

"You're in a salon, everyone share's secrets."

"What makes you think I have secrets?"

Lin giggled... in fact the ladies in the chairs on either side giggled too.

"Now please place both hands under the UV light and hold still."

Jane lean't forward and placed both hands under the UV light...

"Please sit still for 2 minutes."

I wonder why she kept staring at me! Do I have last night written all over my face?

"Please go and rinse your hands at the sink for me, when you get back we will discuss how pretty you want your nails."

"So how would you like your nails?"

"Light pink with tiny red love hearts."

"No problem Jane."

Lin got to work on Jane's nails, painting a nice soft coat of light pink on each. She then painted on three tiny hearts distributing them in the exact same places, then mirrored on the other hand. No other words were spoken between Jane and Lin. Lin was concentrating. Lin, then gave a coat of clear top on each nail...

"Please place both hands under the UV light, hold still."

Each nail was then wiped with an alcohol swab and cuticle cream was applied.

"Now we massage your beautiful hands."

"Okay! Oh jeez Lin, that's a lot of lotion."

"Well girl, we have plenty of time to chat now."

"You wake up with a hangover?"

"I did yes…"

"You wake up with anything else?"
Oh crap!! Does she know something?
"Did you see me last night?"
"No Jane, but you have secrets, I can tell, I know."
She pointed at me.
"If you must know, I woke up next to a man and I have no clue how."
"Awww girl, you had far too many drinks."
"No shit!"
"This man, is he good looking?"
"I don't know."
"You don't know? Girl you're confusing me."
The ladies on either side were truly engaged in my conversation, the odd gasps with side eye viewing.
"I am confused, which is why tonight is very important to me."
"You meeting him again?"
"No, I have one last hope from someone in the bar tonight to shed light on this man."
"Well Jane, we are all done here, you like your nails?"
"I do, thank you Lin!"

"My pleasure, you come back sometime and tell us more."

Jane just stared at Lin for a few seconds. The ladies on either side started waving bye to her as she made her way to the reception desk.

"That will be £45.00."

Jane paid, and as she opened the door, the two ladies and Lin were shouting out, "Bye Jane, have fun!!! Come again soon! Come tell us about your secret man!"

She left the shop wondering what was being said about her. Jane knows that the ladies and clients will be deciding if she is stupid or not. She imagined the kind of conversations taking place.

"*Oh, how does one not know who is in the bed?*"

"*To think that she left a man in her bed.*"

"*I wouldn't have left the bed with a man's thigh between mine!*"

"*It's a scandal!*"

Although Jane's nails are absolutely pretty, she is feeling rather silly that she revealed her weekend antics to total strangers. She would normally do her nails herself but given the circumstances she had no choice to have someone else do them for her. Jane had no idea how environments like this can cause a client into revealing dark secrets of their life. This of course is not said in a bad way at all, seeing as it is actually very easy to pour your heart out to a friendly face while having your nails done. An esthetician becomes your therapist in a moment of relaxation. Nonetheless, Jane feels completely stupid. She should do too, who does what she does, like... Der!!!

 Time is ticking by, she needs to make sure she is ready for her night. Believe me, what Jane pulls next is an absolute no no!

 "Ok, I need to spruce up my makeup!"

 Jane wanders around aimlessly trying to find a suitable shop to get a touch up on her makeup. As she turns a corner along the highstreet she sees a shop that just might be suitable.

 'Perfected Pouts' hmmm that might be ok for our Jane. She swings open the door, the correct way this time. Enters the shop and starts to look around for the make up she is accustomed to. She sees they have samples for each product but instead of testing them on the back of her hand she does the inevitable we didn't think she would actually do.

Jane decided that she really didn't need to buy a whole new set of makeup as she had enough at home still. She picked up the sample of makeup remover, took some make-up pads and began removing this morning's makeup in front of a tiny mirror on the makeup stand.

"Ma'am, can I help you?" said an assistant.

"I'm good thankyou, just testing your product."

The assistant stepped backwards towards her station but kept an eye on Jane.

Once all the previous makeup was removed Jane stepped over to the concealer. She slightly glanced over to the assistant noting that she was being watched. She applied stripes of concealer across her cheekbones, chin, under the eyes and across her forehead then began rubbing them into her skin. She moved her face side to side in the little mirror to make sure all tired imperfections were hidden. She then took a side step to the foundation section, searched for the one she had at home and dropped a blob of the sample into the palm of her hand.

"Ma'am? Are you doing your makeup?"

"Nope! I am testing the merchandise."

"It looks like you are doing a full makeup cover."

"Lady!!!! I am not spending my money until I know this goes well with my skin, so back off!!!"

The assistant again steps back to her station. Jane, rubs the blob between her hands then applies it all over her face rubbing it in. The assistant starts to step forward again but Jane paused and stared at her making the assistant instantly retreat back.

Next, Jane finds the face powder sample, and puffs it all over her face. I cannot believe that she is forgetting that millions of others have used this same face pad on the back of their hands.

Unbelievably She finds a sample eyeliner, surely she isn't going to use the sample! But yes she actually does. Standards Jane, please remember your standards. Jane, leans right up close to the mirror applying that perfect line to the bottom eyelid, then applies to the top. I cannot imagine the amount of germs on that one eyeliner alone.

"Ma'am, will you please stop?"

"Will you please leave me alone?"

"You cannot do this miss…"

"Who said I can't?"

"Ma'am…"

"Oh bugger off!!!"

Jane shooed her away with the flick of her wrist and continued applying the blusher and lipstick and mascara. She then found the spritz sample and sprayed her face securing her finished makeup.

The assistant frowned as Jane walked past with a huge smile on her face, satisfied with her accomplishment of not spending any money yet looking like a million dollars!

"Ok, I need a bite to eat then off to the bar! Actually I could eat at the bar! Damn, I need to get changed!"

Jane headed for the shopping mall with her bags and entered the public bathrooms. Picked her cubicle and wiggled into her new dress. Put on her new shoes. Placed her purse, tissues and keys into her new bag and flung the strap over her shoulder.

"Hmm, what am I going to do with these clothes? Oh I know!"

She headed towards her home and tucked the bag behind her outside bin. At least no one will think of looking there.

Ok Jane, this is it!!! This is where the final puzzle piece finally gets put into place.

Chapter Six

Is this the end of the story?

Jane re-entered the 'Shaker & Slice' bar. It was already packed out, music blaring. Jane approaches the bar.

"Hi! Can I have a burger and chips please?"

"Sorry what? You will have to speak up!"

"Can I have a burger and chips please?"

"Sorry love, we don't do burgers, you can have a plate of chips though!"

"Yes please!"

"Would you like anything to drink with that miss?"

"Yes, I would like the Shaker & Slice Special!"

"Coming up, miss."

Jane took a seat at the bar.

"Here you are miss, chips and a special."

"How much?"

"£25.00."

"This is really tasty. What is in this?"

"Vodka, rum, gin and a splash of orange juice."

Jane ate her chips and drank her first drink of the evening slowly, previous alcohol had worn off. *"Better pace myself, I have a couple of hours before Terry & Natasha get here. I cannot be pissed as a fart too soon."*

"Another special please!"

"£18.00 please."

"Keep the change sunshine"

"Hey Jane."

"SASHA!!!"

"I thought I would come back to support you."

"Thank you, I'm nervous."

"You, Jane, nervous?"

"Well Der!!! I don't know these people, no idea where we went, ugh! This is actually quite a mess."

"You think?"

"Two specials please!"

"Here you are ladies." Jane pulled the money from her purse and paid.

"What's in this Jane?"

"Don't you worry, just drink."

"So, how are you going to approach these people?"

"Front on Sasha, front on."

"Oh boy, I hope you find out, Is the man still in your bed?"

"No clue…"

"Wait, you still haven't been home yet?"

"Nope!"

"Well, where did you get your clothes from? And how did you do your makeup?"

"I bought my new clothes, and I used the makeup in the store!"

"You bought more makeup?"

Jane stared at Sasha…

"Please tell me you didn't use the samples…"

Jane twisted her lips then stared at her drink. Sasha shook her head.

"You know how many germs are on those?"

"Uh huh!"

"You gonna warn any man you kiss tonight you have germs all over your face?" Sasha giggled.

"Really Sasha? I am on a mission that doesn't include any other man!"

"Seeing is believing I guess!"

"Two specials please!"

"£36.00 ladies."

"Seriously, what is in this drink? it's going to my head already!"

"Lot's, just keep drinking!"

"Hey ladies, would you like a drink?"

"Absolutely not! We cannot have any interruptions right now."

"Okay, okay…" as the man backed away.

"WOW Jane!!! You are on a mission!"

"I told you, I need to get to the bottom of this!"

"Hahaha, there is a bottom in your bed and you might actually end up settling down!"

"Who are you kidding Sasha, I like my freedom!"

And in walks Terry & Natasha…

"Jane look, there they are!!!"

"Ok, keep cool, let's get another drink and give them time to sit down."

"Two specials please!"

"£36.00."

"I will pay for these Jane"

"Cheers Sasha!"

"Oooooh!!! This is it Jane!"

"Keep your cool, they are not far from us!"

"This is exciting!"

"Maybe for you Sasha… Okay, wait here, keep my place at the bar!"

Jane kind've walked over to Terry & Natasha, she was just a little bit tipsy. Thankfully all the walking around and food had sobered Jane up a little…

"Excuse me, do you remember me last night?"

"Oh hi Jane, how are you?"

"Good good, I just have a question for you."

"Sure, fire away!"

"We left the bar last night at 11:15 pm, where did we go?"

"We didn't actually go anywhere."

"We didn't?"

"No, as soon as we got outside we had no plans to go for anymore drinks."

"Hmmmm… Did you see a man?"

"I don't know what to say Jane, we were leaving the car park, a man was heading towards you, why is this important?"

"Have you ever seen this man before?"

"No Jane."

"Did I look happy?"

"You were smiling!"

"Was he good looking?"

"Well, one man's meat is another man's poison!"

"What is that supposed to mean?"

"What's good for you might not be good for me!"

"I wonder if anyone else saw me with him."

"What's going on Jane? Why all the questions?"

"Believe me, you really don't want to know…"

"Actually we do!" Terry said.

"It's ok Jane, you can tell Natasha anything!"

"Look, it's simple, I woke up this morning with a man in my bed."

Natasha spat her drink out…

"So what is wrong with that?"

"I don't know how he got there…"

Terry patted Jane on the back.

"Well done, well done!"

"Wait!!! You woke up in the same bed as him, and you don't know who he is?"

"I don't!"

"How is that even possible?"

"Because, I left him in my bed and have not been home all day!"

Natasha burst into laughter!

"Are you freakin serious? Go home and see if he is still there!"

"I need to find out who he is first!"

"Who cares!"

"Here Jane, I bought you a drink!"

"Thanks Sasha."

"So how is the mission going? You found out who he is?"

"No Sasha, apparently an unknowing man came over to me in the car park."

"Well, you couldn't have come back into the bar, I was in here until 2 am!"

"Great Sasha…"

"What? Do you remember coming back in? Cause I never saw you."

"Wait!!! There were empty bottles on my coffee table this morning!!!"

"What?"

"We must've grabbed some drinks from the bar and…"

"You both went to your house!"

Jane was feeling defeated, she was no closer to finding out who this man was.

"You know what Sasha, I'm going to go home."

"YAY!!!" They all cheered.

"Yeah yeah you lot"

"Well good luck! Hope he is everything you hope him to be" As Terry hugged her.

Jane threw back her drink, and left the bar dragging her feet down the street.

"Jane!!! Jane!!!"

"Who the shit is calling me now?"

"JANE!!!"

"Oh no! Is that…"

An old friend from school was running up to Jane screaming her name out, arms flailing.

"Jessica? Is that you?"

"Yes yes Jane, so good to see you!"

"What are you doing out here?"

"Have you seen my brother?"

"How would I know who your brother is?"

"My brother is such a darling, and you kissed him in 3rd grade!" Jane screwed her face up.

"Still the same Jessica right? I have no clue what your brother looks like."

"Oh he is tall, dark hair, quite a handsome man."

"Uh huh! Nope, not seen any tall men Jessica!"

"Will you help me find him?"

"No! I am going home!"

"Oh please Jane. By the way, we should totally hang out sometime!"

Jane carried on walking, with Jessica doing a partial dance trying to keep up with her.

"Please, just leave me alone…"

"Sweetie, I don't know what to do. Could I at least use your bathroom? I have been walking up and down the streets for the last 2 hours!"

"Go look in the bars."

"He was out with friends last night!"

"That's what most men do Jessica."

"I promise, I will use your bathroom then leave, but do take my number sweetie!"

"Ugh fine."

Jessica followed Jane all the way home. Jane unlocked her door, kicked off her shoes, threw down her handbag and headed towards her bedroom. Jessica followed…

"The bathroom is right there."

"Thank you sweetie, thank you!"

Chapter Seven

The actual end of Friday night!!!

"Hey Natasha, are you going to another bar?"

"No Jane, me and Terry are going home now."

"Awww you don't want another drink?"

"Sorry Jane, you shouldn't have anymore either."

"Well, I'm just gonna sit right here on this bench."

"Ok Jane, have fun, nice to meet you, see you around!"

"Yeah see ya!"

Jane's head was so woozy, the drone of music was still pounding in her ears. She had no energy or balance to walk far.

"OI! Girly!!!"

Jane glanced up to see this man swaying side to side making his way towards her.

"Well look what we have here!" He said with a massive grin.

"*Well hello gorgeous!!!*" Her mind narrated to herself.

"Hi, what's your name, pretty lady?"

"You're so sweet, it's Jane and yours?"

"You can call me handsome."

"Well nice to meet you handsome!"

"Yeah, yeah nice to meet you Jane, why are you sitting outside?"

"Ugh, it's been a busy night! I thought I was going to another bar, but I seem to be sitting here, and why are you sitting here?"

"Well I'm sitting with you! OMG your hair!!!"

"What about my hair? Is it fucked?"

"No, nooooooo, nooooooo, it smells AMAZING!!!"

"Well thank you!"

"So, you want to get another drink?"

"Sure!"

"Wait here Jane, wait, what ya drinking?"

"The bar's special!"

"Don't move, don't vanish, just sit tight you lovely lady, I will be right back! Then I can have a chat with your hair."

"Huh!" Jane wondered if she heard right.

Handsome staggered along the wall trying to find the door…

"Oh wow! Go along a bit more, you're getting closer to the door!"

"Am I there yet?"

"Nooo, a bit more to your right."

"This way? Am I there yet?"

"Oh blimey! Yes, just a tad more! Now feel for the door knob!"

"Got it!!! Thank you Jane!"

Jane sat patiently waiting for her handsome man to get back… And waited… And waited…

"Oi Jane, come 'ere!"

Jane wobbled a little but eventually made it to her feet. She ran her hand along the wall to help balance herself.

"Jane, my lovely, come inside and help this poor chappie!"

"What are you doing?"

"Just hold the door open, love."

"What do you have there?"

"Hold on, let me grab the bag!"

He had bought so much drink for them both, with no knowing where they would even end up.

"Wait, wait, wait, hold the door again Jane…"

He reached in, and picked up two flasks filled with the bars special on ice.

"See, we can drink this one while we walk!"

"What's in this?"

"A full flask of the special drink!"

"Well if my socks weren't completely knocked off yet, they sure will be!"

"You're funny too!" He smiled.

"So what's in the bag?"

"I don't know, I asked them to surprise us with drinks and snacks."

He flung his arm around her shoulders…

"Where we off to?"

"Not sure yet, let's go in that direction." Jane kind've points randomly.

"Sounds good… Let's go!!!" He shouted.

They both swayed around bouncing back into each other while sipping through the flask straws.

"Jane? Are we back where we started?"

"Oh, oops hahaha, let's go in THAT direction!"

"Wahoo! Here we go again girl!"

Staggering down the road they eventually came close to Jane's house…

"Girl, I seriously need to take a leak!"

"Tie a knot in it!"

"I did that ages ago, it's ready to burst!"

"We are near my home, but I need to go to bed."

"Ahhh come on Jane, let a man have a leak…"

"I don't know, I don't normally allow men in my home."

"Hey, Jane!!! I'm not just any man, I'm handsome! And you're lovely and we still have all this drink to get through!"

"Ugh fine!!! You can have your leak, we can drink some more, but then I will need to go to bed."

She fumbles her hand around in her bag to find the key.

"Hurry Jane hurry!"

Jane places the key in the door…

"Hurry! Hurry!" He is bouncing up and down desperately needing to use the bathroom.

"I'm trying! Hold the heck on."

"Nope, can't hold any longer!"

Finally Jane gets the door open…

"Where's your bathroom girl?"

"Just down the hall."

He sped off and burst into the bathroom. His voice bellows out…

"Ahhhhhhhhhhh! You have no idea how good this is!"

"I'm sure it's great!" Jane shouted out.

"Oh yeah!!! This is the life!!!"

Jane brought two glasses to the coffee table and waited for him on the sofa.

"OOF! That was great, now, where were we Jane?"

"About to have some more drinks!"

"Yes yes of course, pass me the bag, I will pour us a drink."

"Why were you out alone?"

"I was with a load of mates, but the night ended and I wandered around for a bit until I saw you."

"Special occasion?"

"Nah not really, just a piss up."

"So, why were you out alone?"

"That's hilarious Jane, are you that drunk?"

"I would say so, why?"

"You just asked me that same question 30 seconds ago!"

"Really? Did I?"

"Yep, hahaha!"

"I need to get out of these clothes, I won't be a minute."

Jane hummed to herself a catchy happy tune while she grabbed a few items from the drawers in her bedroom. She took a good look at herself in her long mirror. "*I look hot!!!*" She thought while pointing at her reflection. She staggered back to the living room.

"That's better, that dress was tight."

"Still look absolutely stunning Jane!"

"You're drunk, I'm drunk. We both look beautiful, don't let anyone else say different!"

"Agreed Jane, agreed!"

They stared at each other for a few seconds that seemed like a lifetime to the both of them. "*Mmmm look at this man!*" She thought. Jane lean't towards him, eyes shut, lips puckered ready to lay the first kiss. Their lips glued together, no movement, just two sets of puckered lips touching lips. Just like 3rd grade again. When Jane finally released, they stared at each other again. Jane smiled.

"That was nice Jane, you have a kiss of a thousand kisses."

"Right!!! Your top lip tastes nice, let's do it again!"

"Saucy lady!"

Jane threw her arms around his neck and started snogging him… and snogged…. Ugh, still snogging. Taps fingers!!!

"Wow Jane!!!"

"Mmmm Mr. Handsome…"

"Another drink Jane?"

"Absobloodylutely."

"I like you a lot."

"I like you too Mr. Handsome." As they clinked glasses together.

"Janey Janey, why have we not met before?"

"Maybe we have? Or maybe we have not."

She laid down and rested her head on his leg enjoying all the attention from this hunk of a man in her house! She felt very comfortable, relaxed, and extremely drunk. They both were.

He slid his hand down her top and pressed his fingers into her memory foam boob.

"Wow! Jane! Your boob is amazing!"

"I know!!! You should try the other one. It feels the same as the other one!"

His hand slid over to her other boob. His fingers poked around.

"WOW! Jane! That one feels amazing too!"

He twisted his body around, Jane sat up. He knelt on the floor in front of her and placed one hand on each boob.

"I cannot get over this. Your boobs…"

He wiggled his fingers on each, did tapping motions like playing the piano, and squeezing them intermittently.

"Uh huh! You betcha Mr. I have boobs that every woman wants!"

He prodded them, making sure that they were truly identical.

"No kidding! I want boobs like this!"

They both giggled and knocked back another drink. Jane leant forward and pushed him onto his back on the floor. She straddled him and leant in to kiss him again.

"Omg! Why does your top lip taste so flippin good."

"Well actually…."

"Nope!!! Don't tell me, let me have this night!"

Jane leant in, and kissed him once again. While they were interlocked with each other, Mr. Handsome slowly edged his butt towards the hallway leading to her bedroom. Jane couldn't stop kissing him, the taste of his upper lip was the weirdest taste ever, yet she couldn't get enough of it. Jane kept trying to pinpoint the flavour, but she had no answer, she just had to keep placing her drunken numb lips upon his and keep kissing him until she knew.

As she replaced her lips onto his, and from the jolted movement while he shuffled along the floor, an incy little bit of fluid released from his top lip. It was sour, bitter and something else. *"Is this lip balm?"* She thought. Mr. Handsome flipped Jane over so she was underneath him. He placed his hand under her back and continued to shuffle along the carpet. A slight drip fell upon Jane's lip. She licked her lips, enduring the taste of his so-called lip balm.

They slowly continued to shuffle their way to the bedroom with endless kissing. Jane just cannot get enough of him, and his lip.

As they reach towards her bed, Mr. Handsome stands up, picks Jane up, slaps a firm kiss on her and throws her on the bed! "Let's rock and roll Mr. Handsome."

I think it's time we stayed out of their affairs now. Judging by Jane's morning, we know they had a damn good time.

Chapter Eight

Back to reality!!!!

So, what's next… ahhh yes, Jessica is in her bathroom…

Jane walked slowly to her bedroom, oddly the door had been pushed partially closed, *"Did he leave? Well there is only one way to find out."* She pushed the door open to see if Mr. Handsome was still sleeping in her bed. He is. He is still there. She froze. She didn't know what to do. She stood at the end of the bed staring at this hump under the covers.

Jessica walked into Jane's bedroom…

"There you are!!! Oh and what do we have here? You never said you had a man in your life! Saucy Jane!!!"

"Shh…" replied Jane.

The covers moved…A drowned out voice from beneath asked…

"Is that you Jane?"

Jane didn't know how to respond. She placed her finger over her lip and looked at Jessica, to be quiet.

Part of his hair emerged from the cover. Jane's heart was racing. She didn't know what to expect him to look like. Jessica looked at Jane and mouthed, "Is that Carl?"

"I don't know!!!" She mouthed back.

"What do you mean, you don't know!?"

"I don't remember how he got here."

"Jane, be a babe and get me a glass of water…"

Jane just stared at Jessica shaking her head frantically. She didn't want to speak, or breathe for that matter.

"Babe, are you still here? My mouth is really dry."

As he twisted under the covers, more hair was revealed, more than Jane liked. In fact she started conversing with herself, *"Oh my, that hair! Looks like it needs a damn good wash! I wonder what his face looks like. Hmm not sure, but will soon find out."*

Handsome flung a long skinny arm out of the covers and a smell! Jane's eyes widened. The overwhelming B.O. wafted towards her, filling her room with pure stench. Jessica was looking impatient.

"Babe, babe! I really need water."

"*Why is he speaking like that?*" she wondered. He grunted under the covers, and slowly wormed his way higher in the bed and sat up leaning against the wall. He grabbed Jane's pillow, clutched it close to his chest and sniffed it. Jane instantly became completely sober.

'*Oh fuuuuuck!!!*' Was the only thing going through Jane's mind right now, totally speechless! He has pale skin with a drawn in face and… "*WTF is that on his lip!!!*"

"Carl?" asked Jessica.

"Hi, can someone PLEASE get me a drink of water, my mouth feels like the sahara desert!"

Jane wanted to cry!!!

"Fine! I will get you one." replied Jessica.

Jane looked down at her feet while Jessica went to her kitchen. She didn't want to make eye contact at all…

"You ok Babe? I had a marvelous night with you."

Jane looked at him, cringed and just wanted him to stop talking. His voice was hurting her ears, his overgrown stubble was just… NOPE!!! And there was a huge juicy yellow zit above his lip waiting to burst! And his shoulders looked like he had previously starved himself. As he lowered her pillow she saw the immense amount of hair he had on his chest. His long greasy hair was dangling down towards his nips.

"*OMFG!! His nips are huge!!! Is that even a thing? They could've poked my eyes out!!! What am I going to do?*"

Jessica had enough of the wait…

"So Carl, why are you in Jane's bed? Did you crash here last night?"

"No Jessica, I have been here since Friday night. I have been with lovely Jane!"

"Carl! Bernadette was waiting for you last night!"

"Oops!!!"

Jessica looked at Jane waiting for some form of response. All Jane could do was shrug her shoulders, with no words.

"Hey babe, you want to sit with me? Does your hair still smell good?…"

"No thank you." In a broken voice were the only words to fall out of Jane's mouth.

"Jane, you do know who Carl is right?"

"Not a bloody clue Jessica, how do you know him?"

"Erm, that's my brother, the one you kissed in third grade."

"LA LA LA LA LA" She yelled out with her hands over her ears.

Jane slightly vomited in her mouth with the only option to swallow it again. The zit was staring right at her, it was so huge it was trying to communicate in morse code with her! The one flashback out of the entire Friday night, was her telling him his top lip tasted good! *Did I taste his zit? Grose! And Oh shit! His eyebrows*! They are so bushy!" Jane shudders as the vomit is close to surfacing again. *"What have I done!"*

Jane secretly sent a text…
Jane: Sasha, please come round, and don't judge me.

Sasha: Sorry Jane I cannot right now, is everything ok?
Jane: No, it's not!
Sasha: Hey, tell me all about it later, How is the man? speak soon.

Jane was not about to tell Sasha who this man was in a text.

"*UGH!!! What to do, what to do.* I'm going to pop to the bathroom" she said.

Jane whispered in Jessica's ear, "Please, can you and your brother just leave?"

"Shortly, yes. She replied. I guess we will be seeing you again Jane"

"Nope!" As Jane left the room.

Jane pressed her ear up against the bathroom door. She heard Jessica asking Carl to hurry up and get ready to go. She told him she will meet him outside in five minutes. Jane stayed in the bathroom for the entire time. When she came out, Jessica had already left, but Carl was getting dressed in her bedroom. As Jane got to the bedroom she witnessed Carl's bare arse, bent over, full mooning at her! This wasn't a total eclipse, it was like two half moons spaced apart with a sea of hair. Jane gagged and tiptoed back to the bathroom to give him a few more minutes. But when she re opened the bathroom door.

"There you are babe, you hiding from me? I have left my number on your coffee table, do call me, we had such a good night, love you Jaaane!"

Jane's eyes were squinting at his voice, he leaned forward and laid a kiss on Jane's lips. She could feel the vomit waiting to erupt!

"You're an amazing girl. Can't wait to see you again!"

With that, he grabbed his shoes and met up with Jessica outside. Jane closed the front door and wondered how she was going to tell all her friends about the once perfect man's thigh between hers and she vowed to herself she will never visit 'Tranquil Tips' again! No way could she reveal the results from Friday night.

Jane rushed back to the bathroom and vomited. Washed her face, gargled with mouthwash and applied a mud mask. She changed the bed sheets, picked up her clothes and lit a scented candle to rid the stench then put the kettle on for a hot chocolate. Despite the fact that it was early hours Sunday morning, she got ready for bed, cleaned the mud pack off, made the hot chocolate, took a cover to the sofa and put on 'Bridget Jones Diary'. She had no plans to go anywhere Sunday evening, just to stay at home out the way of all her friends.

Once the film was over, Jane crawled into bed, any sleep was better than none. She tried hard to fall asleep unfortunately everytime she closed her eyes, all she could see was the huge yellow
zit trying to communicate with her. She tried singing in her head, counting sheep and even reciting the ABC song. She thought about a holiday so Jane quickly scrolled through her phone and instantly booked a holiday to Spain! *"Oh a lovely hot beach"* She thought. Time away would be so perfect for her. She so desperately needed to forget this entire weekend. Once she started singing Do-Re-Mi in her head a few times, she eventually fell asleep.

New day for Jane tomorrow, back to work and a booked holiday. Maybe Jane will refrain from drinking too much this coming weekend, I know she will definately not make the ultimate mistake of taking a man back to hers on the night of meeting them. Well, one can hope!

    Poor Jane, how embarrassing, even for her. Sleep well Jane, I'm sure by morning you will be feeling yourself again.

Any names of shops, restaurants or bars mentioned in this book have absolutely no connection with any real places in case any do exist. I spent oodles of time making names up and searching to make sure they did not exist. If I have searched wrong for any place or shop names within this book, it was not intentional but no connection. This book is totally fictional.

Look out for more Stories about Jane!